WHAT I WISH I KNEW ABOUT

abortion

ISBN 9781727897494

Printed in the United States of America.

First printing 2018.

www.chandrajarrett.com

Dedication

I dedicate this book to my first born son Marcus William and in honor of my aborted babies, Marquecia Denise and Malcolm Wesley. I am a better woman, a better mother, and a better person because of my children. May our story encourage others to overcome fear, seek truth, and talk to a loved one before making a choice that can never be changed. With love! Chandra

WHAT I WISH I KNEW ABOUT ABORTION

Contents

Acknowledgements

I've spent the past four years writing and rewriting my abortion story. It was much harder than I thought and I owe a debt of gratitude to the many people who helped me complete this book. I could not have done it without them.

I am eternally grateful for my son **Marcus** who motivates me to be the best me. As his mother, my story is a part of his story and his story is part of my story. Sometimes it's hard to determine where my story ends and his begins, yet he gives me space to share my story to encourage, educate, and empower others. Thank you for the unconditional love, consistent support, ideas, and confidence in me. You are the best gift God has given me. I love you and I'm proud to be your mom.

To **Toby DeBause** and **Wendy Manos**, thank you for believing in me. I've learned more about abortion in the past six years than in my entire life while working with you. I've learned the difference between being pro-life and pro-choice, the importance of educating women about all options, and the need for abortion recovery programs. Thank you for teaching me how to show compassion to all people and how to speak the truth in love without judgement or condemnation. It is an honor to consider you my friends.

To **Torri Edwards** and **Nikki Parker** for helping me write the first draft. Nikki, thank you for watching countless videos of me talking through my story and then writing the draft in way that made sense. Torri, thank you for separating chapters and sections by cutting paragraphs and sentences and then gluing them to poster boards to make my story flow logically. I appreciate you both for patiently encouraging me to keep pressing forward.

To **Christine Robinson** for sometimes gently and other times sternly reminding me that I had a deadline to meet. Your encouragement was always filled with love for me and love for those who could benefit from hearing my story. Thank you for encouraging me to meet with patients considering abortion. Their questions were catalyst for this book. Thank you for being the best cheerleader and coach I could have!

To **Desiree Gaul** for taking time to make edits across the Atlantic Ocean while living in Germany. Thank you for answering my many questions and responding quickly even though we were on a six-hour time difference. I appreciate your honesty, attention to detail, and your ability to help me provide context to my story succinctly. I am grateful for your friendship, support and love. *Leslie Hawkins*, thank you for willingly being an additional set of eyes to edit my story. I appreciate your friendship and love.

To *Patricia Boone* of 823 Creative Co. for designing the book cover. You nailed it with the color, texture and fonts. It's great to have a graphic designer who understands me and can transform the vision in my head to a finished product. You're the best!

And last but not least, to my prayer shield of women who have been praying for the completion of this book, some for years and others as recent as this year. To *Dr. Diane Chandler, Karen DeBause, Torri Edwards, Tonya Epps, Desiree Gaul, Leslie Hawkins, Wendy Manos, Courtney Pickford, Christine Robinson, Rosalyn Thompson, Lisa Woolston,* and *Julie Zimmerman*. Thank you for the texts, phone calls, meetings, wise counsel, and prayers. When I wanted to quit, your prayers were the wind beneath my wing. I am eternally grateful to each of you.

Preface
Why write another book about abortion?

In 1985, I had my first abortion when I was about twenty weeks pregnant. In 1987, I had my second abortion when I was about six weeks pregnant. I spent twenty-five years suffering from the trauma of my abortions. I was not prepared for either abortion procedure. Abortion was offered to me as a solution to my unplanned pregnancies. I do not blame anyone for my decision. I'm solely responsible for the choice I made both times. However, I wish I had been given more information about abortion – before, during, and after the procedure to help me prepare mentally, emotionally, spiritually, and physically.

Why am I writing about my story now? I was healed of post abortion traumatic stress November 8, 2010 while attending an abortion recovery class. After completing the class, I realized I was not provided adequate information about abortion and its side-effects. I've also learned that other women are not always given detailed information about abortion, specifically the procedure and possible side-effects. I have written this book to share the facts about my abortion experiences. My purpose is to make known the various aspects of the abortion process while also providing healing resources for men and women who've had an abortion.

The biggest qualification I have in writing this book is my firsthand experience of a first and second trimester abortion. In addition, I have led post-abortion small groups for seven years. Lastly, I've worked for a pregnancy medical clinic for the past six years that allows me to speak to women considering abortion and women who have had an abortion. I hear the fears, shame, guilt, regrets, and many questions about abortion.

I was frustrated, angry, and sad after my abortions. I had many questions. I didn't understand why I didn't receive more information about abortion. I was completely oblivious of the impact it would have on my life. After hearing this same plight of many women, I realized I could educate and empower other women by sharing my story.

In this book I write specifically about what I wish I knew before, during, and after my abortions. In doing so, I hope to provide insight for each step of the procedure for women considering abortion.

Abortion often changes the course of a woman's life forever. Abortion is a permanent decision that can never be reversed. I believe that it's only fair to know as much as possible before having an abortion.

This book does not answer every question about abortion, nor does it include everything a woman could or would experience with abortion. Again, this book is about my abortion experience and what I wish I knew before making the choice to terminate my children's lives.

What I wish I knew about ROE V. WADE

- I wish I knew Roe v. Wade was and is about terminating the life of a child.
- I wish I knew being pro-choice has nothing to do with my rights concerning the health of body such as my breast, lungs, or heart.
- I wish I knew being pro-choice has nothing to do with my right to vote, or receive equal pay.
- I wish I knew Roe v. Wade took away the legal right for a father to be involved in the decision of his child's life (or death).

At the time of my abortions, I had no understanding about the passing of Roe v. Wade. I was naïve and quite ignorant about abortion. I knew abortion was legal but I knew nothing about the law. It would be twenty-eight years after my first abortion that I began learning about Roe v. Wade. I do not want that to be the same for you or anyone you know considering abortion. I want you to know what I didn't know.

In January 1973, in the case of Roe v. Wade (410 U.S. 113), the Supreme Court "established a woman's right to have an abortion without undue restrictive interference from the government. The Court held that a woman's right to decide for herself to bring or not bring a pregnancy to term is guaranteed under the Fourteenth Amendment." *In other words, a woman's right to privacy gave her the right to terminate the life of her child without the interference of politicians, doctors, family, etc.*

I thought Roe v. Wade was about a woman's health such as my right to choose what happens to my body, i.e. my breast, my lungs, or my heart. I thought the passing of Roe v. Wade protected my right to vote and my right to receive equal pay. Simply put, I thought the passing of Roe v. Wade was an all-encompassing law that protected my rights as a woman. I was wrong, very wrong.

I felt deceived and misled after learning the truth about Roe v. Wade. I felt like the media had intentionally tricked me into believing that being pro-choice meant more than what it means, that it included more than abortion rights.

Merriam-Webster Dictionary defines pro-choice as "favoring the legalization of abortion." A person who is ***pro-choice believes a woman has the legal right to terminate the life of her child; nothing more, nothing less.*** Being pro-choice is directly connected to Roe v. Wade because it supports the legalization of abortion.

Prior to learning the definition of pro-choice, I considered myself pro-life AND pro-choice. I was pro-life because I believed abortion was wrong even after having two abortions. I was pro-choice because I believed a woman had a right to choose what happens

3

to her body. After learning the definition of pro-choice I realized I was not pro-life AND pro-choice, I am pro-life.

In addition, I've since learned being pro-life doesn't mean I give up my rights as a woman. I can be pro-life and fight for equal rights for women, such as voting, equal pay, and health.

Lastly, I was unaware of the impact Roe v. Wade had upon the rights, or lack thereof, of the father of my aborted children. Roe v. Wade allowed me to terminate the life of my child without the father's consent. According to Roe v. Wade, the father has no legal right to prevent a woman from aborting *their* child. The father has no right to protect his child from death and the father has no right to save his child for life. It is the woman's right to privacy, privacy from the father, family, medical professionals, or friend that allows her to terminate the life of *their* child.

The father of my children would not have agreed to abortion and I knew that. Regardless of how he felt, my decision would override his because Roe v. Wade gave me complete legal control concerning *our* children. The same is true today. As a matter of fact in some states a married man cannot prevent his wife from having an abortion because of Roe v. Wade.

It's been more than forty-five years since the passing of Roe v. Wade, four and a half decades. I sometimes wonder if men are less involved in the lives of their children because Roe v. Wade subtly removed their rights to protect and provide for their children. I wonder if some men are absent from families because they don't feel like they have a *legal right* to speak on behalf of their child(ren) because of Roe v. Wade.

Is it fair to legally mandate a man to care and provide for his child after birth while robbing him of his right to protect his child in the womb? I believe every father should be given the opportunity to love, protect and provide for his child before AND after birth.

Every day I regret my decision not to include the father of *our* children in my decision to have an abortion. I regret not having a conversation with him, allowing him to help me in making the best decision for *our* children. I regret not giving him the opportunity to protect *our* children, to save *our* children, and to love *our* children.

In June, 2017, he died without the one thing he wished for –children -- all because Roe v. Wade gave me the legal right to terminate the life of *our* children without his consent.

What I wish I knew about FEAR

- I wish I knew fear over time would create anxiety and lead to depression.
- I wish I knew fear would prevent me from thinking clearly or logically while considering abortion.
- I wish I knew fear would drown out the truth about my situation, causing me to become consumed with "what could happen."

I faced my first unplanned pregnancy at the age of nineteen while completing my sophomore year of college. My menstrual cycle was 3 months late, yet I wasn't concerned because my menstrual cycle was often late. I scheduled an appointment with my doctor as a precaution to make sure I was well. Pregnancy was the furthest thing from my mind because I had never been penetrated sexually.

The doctor recommended a full exam including a urine sample. I complied with everything I was asked to do because in my naïve mind, I was fine. After the doctor examined me and discussed the results with the nurse, the nurse returned to the room and asks me, "Are you going to keep it or not?" I immediately replied, "Keep what?"

Without explanation, the nurse asked the same question with more force, "Are you going to keep it or not?" I became angry because she refused to answer me.

I yelled, "Keep what?!? I haven't done anything! Where is the doctor? I want to talk to the doctor! Keep what?!"

Everyone in the office heard me screaming as I began to panic about the possibility of being pregnant. The doctor returned to the room attempting to calm me down. He explained that I was three months pregnant. When I told him I had not had sexual intercourse, he told me that I could get pregnant without being penetrated. He said, "The penis does not have to be in the vagina for you to get pregnant. Sperm swim"

Sperm swim. I was shocked, confused, and angry. I felt like a fool for not knowing I could get pregnant without having sex. I was speechless.

Nonetheless, I never once considered abortion because I believed terminating the life of a child was wrong, I was shocked to learn I was pregnant and I was nervous about having a child at such a young age, but I was not afraid. I instantly loved my child and I would do anything required to keep it.

I cried on the way home. I didn't understand how this happened to me. I didn't know what my life would be like because my boyfriend and I had ended our relationship in December and it was now March. I was overcome with emotions.

I immediately called my mom when I arrived home. I told her everything that happened at the doctor's office.

She calmly responded by saying, "Yes that's true. Sperm swim. Your cousin was born that way."

I thought, "What?!?! My cousin was born that way and you never told me." She then said, "It's your body and your choice. I'll support whatever you decide."

Why didn't my mother tell me I could get pregnant playing around? What did she mean when she said it's my choice and my body? I felt betrayed, alone, and confused.

I ended the call with my mom and called my ex-boyfriend to tell him I was pregnant. With plans to graduate from college in two months, he was in another state interviewing for graduate school when I called him. We admitted that timing was not perfect however we both agreed we would have our son. He asked me to wait until he completed graduate school to marry but my shame and guilt insisted we get married right away. We married the next month and our son was born a few months later. Unfortunately our marriage quickly went downhill because we were not prepared for the commitment and responsibilities of marriage. He was right. We should have waited.

Sixteen months after saying "I do," I was pregnant a second time but my husband was not the father. I conceived this child by having an affair in a feeble attempt to get revenge from my husband who was having an affair. Even though it was the first time having sex with this man, I knew the moment the condom broke I was pregnant. A few weeks later, the doctor's office confirmed the dreaded truth. I was pregnant by a man who was not my husband.

I was terrified.

I felt like my life was over.

Fear overwhelmed me.

I was afraid of what my mother would say. Would she be as patient with my second pregnancy as she was with my first pregnancy? Would she still love and accept me if she knew my child was conceived by a man who wasn't my husband? Would she love this child as much as she loved my son considering the circumstances?

I was also afraid of what family and friends would think of me, especially those who considered me to be a "good Christian girl." Would they judge me or would they love me? If they knew the truth about my situation, would they still accept me?

I was most afraid of what my husband would do when he found out I was pregnant by another man. I immediately plotted a plan to deceive him but the plan failed. I silently lied by not admitting who the father was. The lies and deception would come back to haunt me years later, causing unnecessary pain to many people, when forced to admit the truth.

Fear paralyzed me so much that I didn't talk to my husband. I didn't talk to my mother. I didn't talk to my family or my friends. I talked to no one. I would never know how anyone felt because I was more afraid of being judged than hearing the heart of those who loved me.

All I could think about was the wrong I had done and the shame I would bring upon my child if I gave birth. Why should my child suffer and be called names because of my wrong doing? How would I live with myself with the embarrassment I brought upon my family?

I was not prepared for the flood of emotions I felt daily. My fears were mixed with guilt and shame. I was afraid of the possibility of being a parent to two toddlers. I was ashamed of being pregnant by another man and I was overwhelmed with guilt for putting myself in a terrible situation. I felt like a failure and a disgrace to God. Facing a second unplanned pregnancy before my son turned one was humiliating.

I felt hopeless. I didn't believe I could recover from my mistake. I refused to allow anyone to help me process my thoughts in a healthy way. I didn't trust anyone enough to share my secret which led to me internalizing my feelings and replaying my thoughts over and over again in my head. Talking to someone would have given me another opinion, another perspective.

I was paralyzed emotionally for months thinking about all the negative outcomes that "could happen" if I had another child. I could not function because of the mess I had made. I slept and cried. I cried and slept. I couldn't eat. I was sad and depressed. Days turned into weeks and weeks into months.

Fear consumed my mind. Fear pained my heart. I was drowning in fear. Fear paralyzed my life and eventually won. I decided to have an abortion when I was almost twenty weeks pregnant.

Why would I wait so long and then terminate my pregnancy? Why would I allow the child to grow in me, knowing there is life there, and still end the life of my child? Fear.

I believed abortion was the only option to overcome fear and relieve the emotional stress. I was wrong. Abortion brought with it the fear of someone finding out about my abortion, the grief of losing my child and the constant regret of my decision. I simply exchanged one kind of fear for another kind of fear with many other emotional stressors.

I could have avoided decades of heartache and pain, grief and loss, had I talked to someone--anyone--about my fears.

What I wish I knew about MY OPTIONS

- I wish I knew I am mother once I conceive regardless of which option I choose.
- I wish I knew I had three options--parenting, adoption, and abortion.
- I wish I knew abortion was the only irreversible, permanent option.
- I wish I knew choosing adoption does not mean I don't love my child.
- I wish I knew my family and friends would support me in raising my children.

There are three options, not two

When I met with the nurse for my first two pregnancies, the question she asked was the same, "Are you going to *keep it* or *not*?" Interestingly, the word abortion was never spoken. After being examined for my first pregnancy, it took her asking me three times before I understood the question. I knew exactly what she was asking me after being examined for my second pregnancy. Without saying the specific words, the nurse was asking, "Are you going to *keep your baby* or have an *abortion*?" (emphasis added by me)

The nurse did not go into details about the meaning of the question no matter how many times I asked what she meant. Neither did she take the time to explain the implications if I chose to "keep it" or if I chose "not to keep it." I was given two options, to parent or have an abortion. As a twenty-something year old girl, either option was a lot to consider. Talking through each option would have been helpful in making the best decision for me and my baby.

My understanding about parenting was the little I knowledge I had from my divorced parents. They weren't perfect but they were both present in my life trying their best to raise five children. I had also babysat siblings, cousins and friends of the family which gave me experience with children. Yet, none of taught me about parenting my own child. I knew raising children was challenging after watching my mother raise five children. I also knew my mother loved us and she had no regrets with having five children.

Unlike parenting, I knew nothing about adoption or abortion. Adoption was not talked about in our home or my school. I didn't know any friends who were adopted. I learned about adoption as an adult.

One would think that I would gain knowledge about abortion after having two abortions. I did not learn about abortion after my first or second abortion. I simply exercised my legal right to choose, my legal right to end the life of my children. I learned about abortion twenty-eight years after my first abortion when I began working for Crisis Pregnancy Center of Tidewater.

I was surprised at how little I knew about abortion even though it was legal and offered to me as an option. I've wondered why the word abortion was never used during my doctor's appointments. Was the nurse afraid of saying the word "abortion?" Was she ashamed of using the word "abortion?" Was she instructed not to use the word "abortion?"

All three options --parenting, adoption and abortion --are difficult options to consider. There are vast differences and outcomes of each option that cannot be determined at the moment of decision. Be that as it may, there are a few things we know about each option.

Parenting

The options of parenting and abortion were offered without an explanation of either. *"Are you going to keep it (parent) or not (abort)?"* The two options were offered as if they were equal in weight and outcome when in reality they are total extremes of each other. If I chose parenting, my child would live. If I chose abortion, my child would die.

Parenting seemed hard because I was young (twenty years old) and my life was complicated (pregnant by a man who was not my husband). Parenting also seemed hard because my first born son was under the age of one. I didn't believe I could handle two children as a single mom. I was also afraid I wouldn't complete college and end up stuck in a dead-end job.

All my life I had watched my family love and support children of family and friends. My mom always allowed people to live with us when they needed a place to stay. She loved everyone in our community, yet I allowed fear to convince me she wouldn't love my children. I never considered the possibilities of parenting my children with support from my husband, the father of the baby or my family. I was afraid and ashamed to talk to them.

I truly believe they would have supported me and helped me care for my children. I believe they would have loved my children equally. I believe with their support and community resources I could have parented two children.

I wish the doctor or nurse had talked to me about parenting. Because they didn't, I live with the regret of having an abortion.

Adoption

Adoption is an option.

Adoption is not permanent.

Adoption is reversible.

The option of adoption was never mentioned to me during any of my pregnancies. I'm not sure why because adoption is a great option to consider when facing an unplanned pregnancy. Over the years I've learned of many families who desire to adopt a new born baby. I may have considered adoption had someone shared information about the benefits of preparing an adoption plan.

Parenting and adoption are similar in that the child's life is not terminated. With both parenting and abortion, the mother has the opportunity to care for, love and watch her child grow.

Adoption would have been hard for me because I would have grieved the loss of my daughter leaving me to be with another family. I would've cried through the process but the tears wouldn't last long because with adoption I could have met my daughter, hugged her, loved her and watched her grow. She could have met her brother, her grandparents, aunts and uncles. Unfortunately, I chose abortion and not adoption.

One might assume "giving away" a child after nine months is harder than terminating a pregnancy at 6 weeks or 20 weeks like I did. I've never made an adoption plan, so I can't say how difficult it is to carry a child for nine months and then entrust her to someone else to parent. I can say that living with the memory of a child who is no longer living inside of you because you chose to end her life is horrible. It is a memory that can never be erased and a decision that can never be changed.

I've heard women say, "There's no way I could carry a child for nine months and then give it away." I understand how difficult that could be after feeling a child growing inside your womb. One of the benefits of adoption is that it's reversible. If a mother makes an adoption plan and changes her mind when she gives birth, she can reverse her decision in many instances and keep her child. She will have the joy of taking her child home, loving and caring for her child. That's not the case with abortion. Abortion cannot be reversed. Once it's done, it's done.

Abortion

Abortion is the only permanent option.

Abortion is the only irreversible option.

Abortion has unexpected and unpredictable outcomes.

Abortion seemed like the best decision because it was a quick solution to my complicated situation. I thought I would feel immediate relief and go on with my life. Not so. I felt immediate regret and suffered for decades from choosing to have an abortion. For twenty-five years I was physically ill, battled depression and cried tears of grief a result of my abortion. I almost died during the procedure, losing so much blood that I had to have a blood transfusion. I was severely depressed so much so that my mother thought I needed to be admitted to a mental hospital.

I never considered the fact that once I terminated the life of my child, I will never see my child. I will never be able to hold my child, hug my child or love my child. I will never be able to watch my child grow up. I will never see a picture of my child. I will never experience my child's high school or college graduation. I will never experience my child getting married or having children.

Choosing to have an abortion is much different than choosing to parent or make an adoption plan because abortion is the only irreversible decision. There is no turning back or changing the outcome after an abortion. Abortion is permanent.

I chose abortion because it was quick and convenient but the after-effects are the opposite of the quick and convenient. Thirty-three years later, the lifelong effects continue to painful and inconvenient. Abortion almost destroyed my life. The emotional, physical, and mental stress was worse than anything I could have imagined. After living with the pain and regret of two abortions, I would much rather see my child cared for by loving parents, than to be tormented with the memory of my child who never lived.

Parenting, adoption, and abortion are difficult options from which to choose. Each path comes with its challenges unique to the person making the decision. My abortion came with a myriad of challenges and regrets. I wish I could reverse my decision but I can't. It is final.

Once a mother, always a mother...

A woman who chooses to parent is a mother.

A woman who makes an adoption plan is a mother.

A woman who chooses to have an abortion is a mother.

Motherhood begins at conception. Science has proven that life begins when the egg and sperm join together at conception. In that miraculous moment, the chromosomes of the mother and father form a tiny cell that contains every detail of the child --eye color, hair color, fingerprint, gender, height, and skin color. One cannot deny these facts.

Some women choose abortion to avoid being a mother. In denying the truth women are sometimes told that the cells are not a baby, they're just a blob of tissue. I believe most women know she has a baby growing inside of her. If she didn't believe it why would she take a pregnancy test to prove or disprove it?

I knew I was a mother each time I conceived. Having an abortion did not change the fact that I was the mother of the child in my womb. I'll admit it was hard accepting the fact that I was a mother at such a young age but I never doubted there was a child inside of me.

I believe most women know they are a mother at conception, which is why having an abortion is traumatic. Our DNA has intertwined with the DNA of our baby, and even though the full body has not formed, we know there is life there. Seeing the blob of tissue as a child is passed in a commode from terminating the pregnancy, or hearing the suction machine as the child's body parts are removed from the mother, or lying in a hospital to birth a dead baby is painful for a mother to watch, even when she's made the choice to do it.

I've heard stories of women who denied being a mother at the time of their abortion but acknowledged the truth after becoming pregnant again later in life. Abortion does not erase or eliminate a woman being a mother to her child. Abortion makes us the mother of a child we will never see, a child we will never hold, and a child we will never watch grow up in this world. Will a mother forget her child based on the options she chooses? NEVER!

Once a mother, always a mother...

What I wish I knew about
THE ABORTION PROCEDURE

- I wish I knew I would begin grieving before, during, and after the abortion procedure.
- I wish I knew I would experience pain during and for days after the procedure.
- I wish I knew I would have memories of the procedure for the rest of my life.
- I wish I knew certain sounds, like a vacuum cleaner, would remind me of the abortion equipment.

Preparation

How does one prepare a woman to terminate the life of her child? What do you say to a mother to prepare her mentally and emotionally to end the life of her child?

"You will be relieved once this is over."

"Your life will be better."

"You can go on with life once this is done."

"You can pursue your career without another child hindering you."

"No man will want you if you have children by two different fathers."

The last three statements were spoken to me when I sought counsel about having my second abortion. I have not found any truth in these statements since my abortions.

I was not relieved after my abortion was over. I was heartbroken, suffering with shame and guilt as I faced the reality of taking my child's life. I did not feel better. I felt worse. And I could not go on with my life. I hated myself for what I had done and the grief paralyzed me. I spiraled into deep depression, crying almost daily the first two years after my abortion and often missed work, unable to function. It is true I only had one child to care for but the heartache, depression, and sickness after my abortion left me with much regret.

I'm not sure how to prepare a woman for the wave of emotions she will feel after an abortion. If you or someone you know is considering an abortion, I'll warn you by saying there will be many unexpected emotions and side effects. Your heart, your mind, and your soul will respond to the loss of child being unnaturally forced out of your body before birth. You may experience emotions you never knew you had. There may be numbness, quiet anger, disappointment, or relief. There may be random outbursts of tears, feelings of grief, loss, or denial. Abortion impacts each woman differently. I've yet to talk to a woman who wasn't emotionally affected by her abortion. Be aware and beware.

My Second Trimester Abortion

I was almost twenty weeks pregnant when I had my first abortion. I had to be hospitalized to induce labor because I was too far along to perform the procedure at the doctor's office. Once admitted, I was placed on a bed and taken to my room where the procedure would take place. As they rolled me down the hallway, I noticed there was no one in the other rooms. The ward was an eerie quiet, almost spooky.

Once in my room, the nurse began the medication to induce labor. It was a beautiful fall day the week of Thanksgiving. The walls were plain, not a picture in sight. The room was quiet with the exception of the IV drip. I remember watching the clock and looking out the window as cars drove up and down the street.

I didn't know what to expect, so I patiently waited for the medication do its thing. After about an hour, I began experiencing severe pain. It felt like a cramp in my stomach with one thousand pounds of pressure. I rubbed my stomach to ease the pain but it only grew worse. In that moment I understood why I was on a ward by myself. The doctor knew the pain I would experience and he knew I would disturb the other patients.

As the pain increased, I began screaming at the top of my lungs, crying for help. I cried and screamed for what seemed like hours but no one came to help me. The pain was so bad I thought I was dying. No one --not one person --told me I would experience pain much less severe pain. Why didn't they tell me what to expect or at least mention the labor pains? I still get angry thinking about the medical neglect of not telling me what would happen to me during the procedure. It's wasn't right and it surely wasn't ethical.

After some time had passed, the doctor and two nurses returned to the room. The doctor positioned himself at the foot of the bed with one nurse beside him while the other nurse stood on the right side of the bed near my waist. They instructed me to push and after the third push the baby came out. The doctor handed the baby to nurse near him who said, "It's a girl." I looked up quickly to see her little body and black hair as the nurse rushed out of the room with her. I will never forget seeing my baby girl that day.

I must have blacked out after they took the baby because I don't remember the remainder of the procedure. When I awoke later, I was told that I had to have a blood transfusion, three pints to be exact, because I lost so much blood during the procure. *A blood transfusion? What?!* In other words, I could have died having an abortion at twenty weeks. Why wasn't I told about the risk? How was this legally allowed?

Women have actually died during the abortion procedure. It's not often discussed but it's true. Abortion can be lethal to both mother and baby. I'm sad and disappointed with myself for not knowing the laws, the risks or any details about the abortion procedure. At the same time, I'm glad to be alive to tell my story in hopes that women will gather as much information as is available before considering an abortion to avoid pain, suffering and possible death.

My First Trimester Abortion

Let me begin by saying that choosing to have a second abortion seemed easier than choosing to have my first abortion. I wrestled for months before deciding to have my first abortion. It only took weeks to make decision for my second abortion.

The truth is I already felt like a failure after having my first abortion. I had taken the life of one child, what was one more abortion? By the time I faced my third unplanned pregnancy, my life had spiraled out of control. I was an emotional wreck. My marriage had fallen apart and I was struggling to graduate while caring for my son. I felt unstable so I sought the counsel of the pastor of the church I attended. In my deep despair, I still wanted to please God.

I told the pastor I was pregnant by a friend and my divorce was not final. I would graduate in a few months and begin my career as an engineer. He listened and then strongly recommended I have an abortion for two reasons. The first reason he presented was having a second child could hinder my careers as a single mother. He explained the many responsibilities of a mother and went on to say that having two children could delay my career.

The second reason he recommended I have an abortion was because "No man will want you if you have children by two different fathers." He made it sound like I would be a single mother the rest of my life if I had two children by two different fathers. I trusted his counsel, heeded his counsel, and had a second abortion.

The thought of his counsel still bothers me. I'm sad to say there are countless pastors like him who would recommend an abortion today. They believe a woman's right to choose supersedes God's Word. For this reason abortion has become a political issue rather than a moral issue. Women are confused whether to obey God or obey the pastor. Sadly, countless women like me have followed the recommendation of their pastor to have an abortion only to find myself silently suffering in guilt and shame. What's the hardest part of following the pastor's recommendation? Receiving God's forgiveness and forgiving myself.

The Lobby

I was a little more than six weeks pregnant when I had my second abortion. Entering the abortion clinic for my appointment was not like going to the doctor's office. The environment was different. It was solemn, quiet, and emotionally weighty. The air was so thick you could cut it with a knife.

I avoided eye contact with anyone when I arrived for my appointment. I was ashamed of being there so I tried to be invisible to others. There was no conversation in the lobby with the exception of someone speaking as she checked in or checked out. I remember looking down the entire time as I waited for my name to be called.

I can still see the machine positioned to the left of my left leg as I lay on the bed. The room was painted a pale tan color with no pictures on the walls. The small room had just enough space for the bed, equipment, and necessary staff.

The doctor sat on a stool between my feet and the nurse stood to the right of my head. The humming of the suction machine was the only sound other than the short conversation before the procedure. I was given anesthesia to numb my vagina area and to keep me calm. The anesthesia helped some, but I felt the painful suction throughout the entire procedure.

The doctor and nurse left the room as I recovered. I was alone for thirty to forty-five minutes. It was during recovery that I felt the initial wave of emotions. It's hard to describe the initial feelings after an abortion. There was shock, disbelief, and denial mixed with disappointment, heartache, and relief. My outer shell felt like a robot going through the motions while my insides felt like an oceans experiencing a tidal wave rising and falling over and over again - heartache, relief, regret, denial, shock, disappointment. Between the emotions, tears quietly ran down my face. I remember going home in pain asking myself "What did you just do?" yet not saying a word to anyone.

One would think the suction procedure of a first trimester abortion would be easier and less painful than a second trimester abortion. Not really. I was in pain during the procedure and for weeks afterwards. I spotted for days, which was considered normal and the pain, well they said it would go away eventually. The pain subdued after a few weeks but who wants to be in pain for weeks especially after being told the procedure would be easy?

The sound of hearing my baby sucked out of me is a memory I carry today. I can still hear the suction machine in the room like it was yesterday. Over the years, the sound of a vacuum cleaner reminds me of the suction machine. I will never forget this experience.

Recovery Room

I recovered in the room of my procedure but I know women who were taken to a recovery room filled with beds of other women who were also recovering from their abortion. One friend told me she quietly cried as she lay on the bed in recovery. She could hear other women crying, some quietly, others much louder.

Another friend said she felt lost and confused as if she

was having an out of body experience. Recovery is

another layer of the procedure that no one talks about

yet it marks us for life.

What I wish I knew about
TRAUMA AND TRIGGERS

- I wish I knew hearing the word "abortion" would trigger feelings of guilt, shame, and regret.
- I wish I knew seeing an ultrasound picture of a baby would trigger memories of my abortion.
- I wish I knew I would get physically ill and deeply depressed after having an abortion.
- I wish I knew driving by the hospital and clinic of my abortion would immediately awaken and replay the details my abortion.
- I wish I knew there was a possible link between abortion and breast cancer.

Merriam-Webster defines trauma and triggers in the following ways:

- **trauma** as a) a disordered psychic or behavioral state resulting from severe mental or emotional stress or physical injury and b) an emotional upset.
- **trigger** (verb) - to cause an intense and usually negative emotional reaction in (someone)

I experienced trauma and triggers for twenty-five years after having two abortions. I am no longer traumatized by my abortions but I continue to experience triggers from my abortion experiences. Here's how abortion affected my emotional, mental, spiritual and physical state of being.

Emotional trauma (before abortion)

The thought of having an abortion drove me to isolation. I didn't want anyone to know I was pregnant by a man who was not my husband. I stopped talking to family and friends because I was disappointed and ashamed of myself. In my mind, I believe they were disappointed an ashamed of me too. I convinced myself no one would understand my struggle in trying to decide whether or not to have an abortion.

I was afraid of being rejected, judged and not loved for being pregnant a second time. I couldn't bear the thought of my child being labeled as a "bastard child" or being taunted because she was conceived from an affair. I truly believed having an abortion was best for my child because I would protect her from the pain I caused.

My husband and I separated within months of my learning of my second pregnancy. I moved back home with my mom and my siblings. My family probably thought I was sad because my marriage was failing.. However, the heaviest burden I was carrying was being pregnant by another man.

I spent most of my time in the bed, day and night. I barely attended classes and my sisters helped with my son because I wasn't emotionally fit to do much. I cried all the time. I wanted to disappear, to die in my sleep. I hated my life and what I had done.

I didn't want to have an abortion, but I wasn't strong enough emotionally to make the decision. I was too ashamed and afraid to talk about it, so days turned into weeks and weeks turned into months. Eventually my thoughts of condemnation, failure, and rejection won. I had the abortion when I was twenty weeks pregnant.

Emotional trauma (after abortion)

Yet again, I was not prepared for the abortion side-affects. The doctor failed to mention the emotional trauma I could experience. There was no mention of heartache, no mention of sickness, no mention of depression, no mention of guilt or shame.

As I lay in the hospital bed after my abortion, not a minute went by that I didn't think about what I had done. All my life I had wanted a daughter. As a matter fact, I had chosen a name for her while still in high school – Marquecia Denise, and now she was gone. Hearing the nurse say "It's a girl" felt like someone has stabbed me in the heart.

Questions raced through my mind...

What have I done?

What if this was the only daughter I'll ever have?

How will I live with myself knowing what I've done?

By the time I arrived home I was deeply depressed. I was depressed about having an abortion and even more depressed knowing it was a girl.

I was sad before my abortion because in my heart I didn't want to have an abortion. I was convinced abortion was the best decision for my complicated situation. I was wrong. It turned out to be the worst decision I've ever made in my life. I didn't know what to do with the anger, depression, sickness and grief I experienced. I couldn't get out of bed most days. My family didn't know how to help me. No one could help me. I was emotionally paralyzed grieving the loss of my child. Sadness was quickly joined by sickness as my body began to exhibit signs of trauma.

Physical trauma

I became physically ill within weeks of my first abortion and it continued for twenty-five years. The sickness would begin as a headache which was followed by vomiting, diarrhea or both. As the sickness became worse I would go from the bedroom to the bathroom where I spent many nights sleeping on the floor.

I still have memories of being sick in a hotel when I began my career as an engineer. I had been accepted into a dual program with a prestigious global corporation. My son and I were staying in a hotel until we found an apartment. The stress of moving and starting a new job caught me by surprise and I became sick. As I lay in bed, my toddler son got the trash can out of the bathroom and brought it to me. He then sat quietly watching television as I began vomiting. I can only imagine the trauma my son experienced watching me go through the trauma of my abortion. It breaks my heart to know my son suffered *with me* unable to enjoy his childhood because of my abortion.

My family learned to give me space when I was sick. It was scary for everyone because no one knew how or why I got sick. I would go to the doctor but by the time I went the trauma had ended and my body returned to normal. As a result no doctor was able to diagnose the sickness. I missed countless hours of work, vacations, family time, and life as a whole.

Spiritual trauma

Life was not perfect before my abortion but I enjoyed it. I did well academically in college and participated in various organizations on campus. I spent time with family and friends and loved going to church. Jesus was my best friend and I told Him everything.

After my abortion, I was not a happy person. I was angry, sad, and afraid that God would never forgive me. I felt like I had failed as a student, as a mother, and as a

Christian. I changed so much after my abortion that I could barely recognize myself, yet I didn't know how to change back to the person I was. I would soon learn abortion changed me never to be the same again.

I was functionally depressed, simply going through the motions of life. I was a ticking time bomb at home, at work, and in relationships. I avoided people as much as possible, hoping no one could see the shame, the pain and regret. I was convinced God would never forgive me for taking the life of my children and I lived as if I had died with them.

I would say to myself, "Jesus doesn't love me anymore and He will never forgive me for what I've done." Yet I wouldn't stop attending church. Somehow in the back of my mind I hoped I was wrong. I hoped that Jesus still loved me and would forgive me as I had learned in Sunday School as a little girl. I hoped Jesus would forgive me of all my sins, even murder.

I overworked and overcommitted myself at church in an attempt to pay penance to God for my abortions. I repented of my sins and felt forgiven in the moment but the guilt and shame would return within days and I was back to working for forgiveness again. Eventually I became burnt out, resentment, and living a life of sexual sin.

In time, I would receive forgiveness and healing from Christ in a post-abortion recovery group. I now carry the memory of my abortion, but I no longer carry the weight of shame and guilt. I am free!

Abortion and Breast Cancer

The first time I enrolled in a post-abortive small group breast cancer was listed on the intake form under "Physical Manifestations" along with miscarriage, stillbirth, cervical pain, and sterility. I didn't think much about breast cancer because I knew very little about cancer and I never thought it being connected to abortion in any way.

Over the years I would learn of family, friends and colleagues who were both post-abortive and breast cancer survivors. I was concerned but not alarmed by this until I was diagnosed with Stage 3 breast cancer June 26, 2015. I immediately recalled the question on the intake form and wondered if I had breast cancer because of my abortion.

While going through treatment, I began researching abortion and breast cancer. I learned that Europe and China have completed studies showing a correlation between abortion and breast cancer. (www.bcpinstitute.org) The "Hush" Documentary also discussed the link between abortion and breast cancer in an attempt to find the truth about abortion and women's health. (www.hushfilm.com)

There seems to be a link between abortion and breast cancer however without more research, I cannot affirmatively say what that link is. I sometimes wonder how many, if any, lives have been lost by breast cancer rooted in an abortion. I wonder how many lives could be saved if we knew the truth about the link between abortion and breast cancer. I wish the USA would conduct an extensive, unbiased study about abortion and breast cancer. Cancer is deadly; don't we deserve to know the truth?

Grief

I thought about my first abortion every day for the first two years. Some days it was all I could think about. I would replay the procedure in my mind and weep for hours. I tried to sleep the memories away only to wake up to the thoughts again. I felt haunted by my abortion and the thought of losing my baby girl.

After the first two years, I buried the memory of my abortion to move forward with my life. The grief was interfering with my career so I had to pull myself together to care for my son. I rarely thought of my abortion if at all, however, the tears continued for different reasons. I cried if someone else was sad, or hurting, or sick. I cried when I prayed for others or if I watched a movie. I became overly sensitive to heartache and pain without knowing that it was connected to my abortions.

After crying for twenty-five years for what seemed like unknown reasons, I entered an abortion recovery class and learned that I was crying tears of grief for the loss of my children. I did not expect to be grieving nor did I know that women grieved the loss of their child after an abortion. In my mind, I didn't think we had a right to grieve after an abortion considering we chose to take the life of our child. My mind was filled with questions.

Why would we grieve something we chose to get rid of?

Why does our heart ache so deeply when we abort our children?

How does a woman grieve her child after an abortion?

How does a family member or friend respond to a woman grieving her abortion?

I never considered the fact that our heart, mind and body experience the loss when we abort our child just as it does in the case of any other death. Logically we know that we had an abortion but our heart, mind, and body is unable to stop the grief caused by the loss.

When friends ask me how to care for someone grieving the loss of an aborted child, I first make them aware of the guilt and shame the person may be carrying. Guilt and shame makes the grief almost impossible to bear. Being sensitive to this fact is important to avoid making the person feel worse.

Each person grieves different reasons and at different times during the grieving process. For example, I initially cried more for the loss of my daughter than I did for the abortions. As time passed and I acknowledged taking the life of my children, I grieved for the wrong I had done. Listening and understanding why she's grieving is important in supporting her as she grieves.

If you've never had an abortion, consider saying, "I'm sorry for your loss. It's okay to grieve the loss of your child." If you've had an abortion, consider saying, "I, too, have had an abortion and I understand the pain you feel. It's okay to grieve the loss of your child." Give the person time and space to share without pressure.

She may not be able to articulate clearly why she's grieving. Be patient. In time she will.

Triggers

I often receive text messages from post-abortive women asking for prayer on either the date of her abortion or the due date of her baby. Why? The date is a reminder of her abortion.

Triggers bring back the memory of a traumatic experience and for each person it's different. Whenever I visit Nashville and drive past the hospital or clinic where my abortion was performed, the memory of the procedure is awakened and replayed in my mind.

Recently I went with a friend to her thirteen week ultrasound appointment for her baby. I sat with her throughout the procedure because the father was unable to attend. As I watched the doctor check for organs and count limbs, I couldn't help but wonder what my daughter looked like at twenty weeks pregnant. That night I dreamt about her baby as I thought of taking the life of mine. I woke up sick to my stomach after being triggered by the ultrasound.

I've met women who are triggered by the word "abortion," attending baby showers, seeing an ultrasound or a newborn baby. Living with the constant memories of an aborted child is tormenting. Jesus Christ came to set us free and I truly believe He can set us free from the torment of abortion.

What I wish I knew about
HEALING RESOURCES

- I wish I knew post-abortive resources were available for women and men.
- I wish I knew I was not the only person suffering from my abortion.
- I wish I knew I could be forgiven and healed from the trauma of my abortion.

I didn't know that resources were available for women and men who have had abortions until 2010. I learned about the class I attended through a friend. I thought it was the only resource until I came on staff at a pregnancy medical clinic (PMC). I've since learned that there are classes/groups, blogs, books/workbooks, and websites to help men and women recover from the trauma of abortion.

People are often surprised when I tell them that our PMC offers abortion recovery classes for women and men. I once asked a woman why she was surprised and she said, "I didn't think you cared about people who've had an abortion. I thought you only cared about babies." I shared the truth by telling her that many PMC's offer abortion recovery classes because we care about the mother, father, and the baby even if the mother chooses to have an abortion.

Prior to entering an abortion recovery group I felt hopeless and alone. I knew I was forgiven but I was not healed, whole or free to live my life. November 8, 2010 I entered a post-abortive Bible study. The first night the Holy Spirit said to me, "There are three things associated with your abortion --your sickness, your crying and your depression." That night I confessed my sin to the small group, and I was forgiven and healed.

Week after week I continued the study about abortion and the weight of grief was lifted. Through the group I learned how to fully process my experience to recover from the emotional, physical and spiritual trauma of my abortion. I still remember the details, but I no longer cry. I still have memories, but I no longer get sick or depressed about my decision. Sometimes I'm sad, and yes, I still regret my decision, but I'm able to live my life as normal as possible with the choice I made.

For twenty-five years I suffered from the trauma of my abortions. For twenty-five years I suffered with grief, sickness, and depression. If someone had told me there were resources available, I would not have suffered for decades. By telling my story I hope to collapse the time of suffering for others.

If you or someone you know is silently suffering from an abortion, consider the resources below. This is not an exhaustive list. There are many resources available today. I hope you or someone you know will find the forgiveness, healing, and freedom many others have found.

Abortion Recovery Resources

Abortion Changes You

www.abortionchangesyou.com

Abortion Recovery International

www.abortionrecovery.org

Option Line

https://optionline.org/after-abortion-support/

Curriculums

Forgiven and Set Free by Linda Cochrane

Healing a Father's Heart by Linda Cochrane and Kathy Jones

Healing Hearts Ministries International

www.healinghearts.org

Her Choice to Heal   www.herchoicetoheal.com

Final Thoughts

Before my abortion, I never considered the fact that a baby growing in my body was a separate person, a baby, another human being who had the same right to life that I have. To terminate the life of my child within my womb was just as wrong as terminating the life of my child outside of my womb. I'm sad to say before understanding this, I believed murder outside of the womb was wrong, yet I supported murder inside the womb. No longer is that the case. I value life equally in the womb and outside the womb.

In closing, here are some of my regrets and lessons learned. I hope they're helpful.

Regrets

- I regret not talking to someone about my thoughts before making a final decision. I had a one-way conversation in my mind that led me to a decision I still regret thirty-two years later. I needed a conversation with someone I trusted to provide information about the pros and cons of all three options. I needed a conversation based on facts not fear, to help me see beyond the immediate crisis.

- I regret not talking to the father of my children before having each abortion. I took the life of his children without allowing him any input in the decision. He desired children until the day he died and I'm left to live with my choice.

- I regret not asking more questions about my options before the procedure.

- I regret choosing abortion without considering all the options – parenting, adoption, and abortion.

- I regret not discussing all the options with my family and/or people who love me.

- I regret ignoring and denying my true feelings about abortion. I didn't believe in abortion and allowed my circumstances to determine my decision, overriding my values and beliefs.

Lessons learned

- Never make a quick decision that has an eternal impact. The first time I had an abortion I took a long time to make the decision because I didn't want to do it. The second time I made a quick decision because I wanted to get it over with. Both times I made a decision without considering the eternal impact.

- Never make a major decision without getting as much information as possible. Do not allow others to rush you. Take time to understand and process the information.

- Never allow fear to have so much power that it rules your life.

- Never suffer silently. Talk to someone -- a friend, a family member, a coworker. More often than not, someone will listen, support you, and help you get the information you need to make the best decision.

- Never allow the opinions of others to dictate your choice. People come and people go. You and only you will live with your decision for the remainder of your life.

Abortion is complex. Abortion has side-effects. Abortion is permanent.

If you or someone you know is considering abortion, take the time to gather the needed information about all options. Talk to someone you trust. Do not allow fear to drive you to make a decision you regret later. You *and your child* deserve to know the facts so you never have to live with the regret of not knowing what I wish I knew about abortion.